BRAIN DETECTIVE

BRAIN DETECTIVE

Investigating Learning

INVESTIGATION IN PROGRESS

STEPHANIE CORCORAN, PHD, NCSP

Illustrated by Rorie Scroggins

LUMINARE PRESS

WWW.LUMINAREPRESS.COM

Brain Detective: Investigating Learning
Copyright © 2021 by Stephanie Corcoran, PhD, NCSP

Printed in the United States of America

Illustrated by Rorie Scroggins

Luminare Press
442 Charnelton St.
Eugene, OR 97401
www.luminarepress.com

LCCN: 2021921517
ISBN: 978-1-64388-812-5

For Quinn & Finley

My name is Lucas. I love pizza, soccer, and my dog, Bo. Bo is my dog's nickname, his actual full name is Bodacious (that's a big word that means brave, bold, and impressive). Bo and I are a bodacious team!

I love using big words (like bodacious) and learning new things at school. But sometimes school is hard for me.

"Bo, I'm having such a hard time at school. I just don't get it. I am doing my best and working so hard. My teacher is helping me, but it is still so tough. I'm beginning to think I might have a bad brain."

One afternoon on the way to soccer practice, my Mom said, "I know you are working really hard at school, but it seems like you are having a hard time and I am not sure why. I have talked with a person at your school who can help us find a way to make school easier for you."

"Really? Who can help us figure that out?" I asked.

"Dr. Sophie" Mom responded.

"Dr. Sophie...Am I sick?" I asked.

Mom responded, "No, you are not sick and there is nothing wrong with you. Dr. Sophie is a different kind of doctor who helps kids learn about their brains. She is like a brain detective who investigates why school is hard for kids. You and Dr. Sophie will do activities together. These activities won't affect your grades at school and many kids say it is fun. We just want to better understand the ways you think and learn. When we know more about how you learn, your teachers and I can find better ways of helping you."

That sounded pretty good to me. I was tired of feeling like I wasn't as smart as the rest of the kids at school. And Bo wanted to spend more time outside playing so we both were ready to solve this mystery!

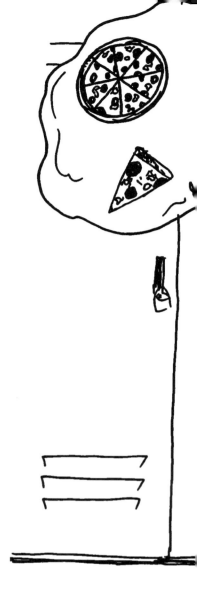

Just as my mom had explained, a nice lady named Dr. Sophie came to my classroom to get me. She was tall, with big glasses and a long ponytail. I whispered to my friends she was a Brain Detective, and they all wanted to come with us!

Dr. Sophie was really fun. It turns out we both love pizza and dogs. Dr. Sophie wanted to hear all about Bo, my soccer team, and how things were going in school. I told her how I am good at soccer, but I have a hard time with school stuff.

Dr. Sophie explained that she was a Brain Detective, and that we would be doing a series of activities together to "investigate" my brain and solve this learning "mystery". She said that the activities give her "clues" about how my brain thinks and learns, and why school is hard for me. She explained that everyone's brain is different. There are no two brains exactly alike. Each one is unique and has special strengths and challenges. She was going to use my "brain clues" to find out what made my brain so special and unique!

Dr. Sophie told me that my job in this investigation was to do my very best. So, I worked bodaciously hard with her.

Some of the activities were simple and fast, some were silly, and some were challenging. Some activities were like what we do in school – math problems and reading words. Some were more fun, like word games, blocks, and puzzles. I really got into these! She also asked me questions, had me say silly words, and I wrote things with a pencil with no eraser. Dr. Sophie wrote notes on her clipboard, while I did the activities. We worked for about an hour and Dr. Sophie gave me a prize when I was finished. Over the next few weeks we worked together several times gathering more and more clues.

After the investigation was completed, Dr. Sophie met with my parents and teachers to explain what she discovered. She revealed that I am very smart, and my brain is organized in a way that makes school stuff more difficult for me. There is nothing wrong with me, I am unique in how I learn.

Dr. Sophie created a team for me. We call it "Team Lucas" and they all help me using the clues we discovered in the investigation.

My schoolwork is improving. It's hard work, but totally worth it.

Best of all, now that I'm doing better in school, I have more time to play soccer outdoors with Bo. I feel bodaciously awesome now that I know how smart and unique I am. Mystery Solved!

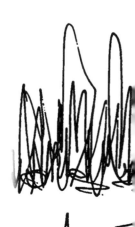

POST-READING ACTIVITY

Think like a detective and gather clues about you!

Fingerprints can provide important evidence in an investigation. Use an ink pad to stamp your fingerprints in the boxes below. Examine your fingerprints with a magnifying glass.

Did you notice any patterns?

Your fingerprints are unique – no one else in the world has the exact same set up ridges and lines that you have. Your brain and how you learn is completely unique to you as well.

INVESTIGATION IN PROGRESS

Write in the magnifying glasses below:

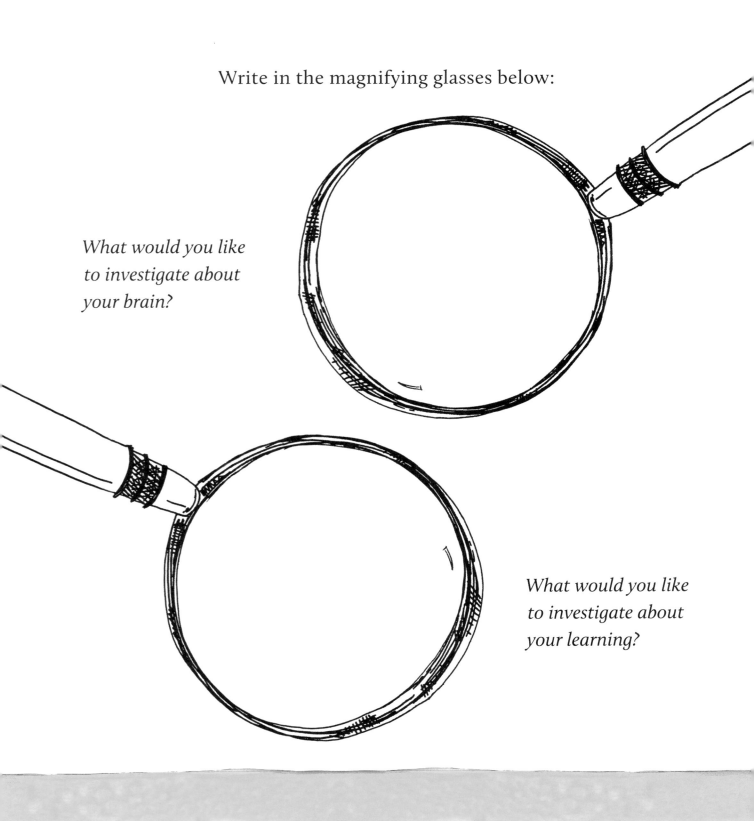

*What would you like
to investigate about
your brain?*

*What would you like
to investigate about
your learning?*

NOTE TO PARENTS

Dear Parent,

In more than 15 years of school-based psychology practice, I have conducted thousands of psychoeducational evaluations. While conducting these evaluations, I consider myself a detective investigating student's barriers to learning such dyslexia, autism, or a number of other learning and behavioral challenges. Such assessments are often a new experience for a family, and I am very frequently asked by parents how they can prepare their children for those evaluations. I have sought "what to expect" books to recommend, sensitive and engaging books similar to the ones I use with my own children and students, but I have not found anything appropriate. As a result, I worry that children and parents go into these assessments with more anxiety and less understanding than is necessary, which could negatively affect outcomes and solutions.

INVESTIGATION IN PROGRESS

So, I created my own book, *Brain Detective: Investigating Learning*, the first in a series that parents, caregivers, and educators can utilize to prepare their children for the psychological evaluation process. My desire is that this book series will help inform children about the evaluation process, alleviate anxieties, facilitate positive open discussions, and empower them with the knowledge and skills to become advocates for their own learning. Once readers meet Lucas, Bo, Dr. Sophie and learn about what brain detectives do, children realize that they are not alone on this journey. I encourage you to first read the "Notes to Parents" section at the back of the book and then read the story with your child. I have provided "Discussion Starters and Talking Points" to get you started. There is also an interactive detective activity that you can complete with your child to foster meaningful positive discussion with your child. Best wishes on your detective mission!

DISCUSSION STARTERS

You may be wondering how to prepare your child for a psychoeducational evaluation. Should your child study for it? What is the best way to talk to your child about what is going to happen? How can you manage your child's worries? There are several things you can do to help you and your child feel more at ease about the evaluation process:

1. Be prepared to talk about the process in an open, positive way. It is helpful to be upfront about what will go on. Explain to your child why they be pulled out of class by a school psychologist or another professional. Most children find the evaluation to be fun – it is not something to be scared of at all.

   "A woman named Dr. Sophie will fetch you from class on Tuesday to do some activities with you. Don't worry! It won't affect your grades at school. Many kids say it is fun. We just want to understand more about the ways you learn."

INVESTIGATION IN PROGRESS

2. Try not to use the term "testing." Assure your child that you cannot study for this and it is not for a grade. Saying that they will do "activities" is less anxiety provoking. Try not to use the term "games" as you do want your child to take the evaluation seriously and do their very best.

"You will be doing some activities like puzzles and answering questions. Many smart kids struggle with school. Sometimes they need extra support or a different kind of teaching to help them do well in school. So, you are going to do some activities to find out more about how you learn and what might help you do your very best at school. The results are really "clues" to give us direction for ways to help you learn."

3. Explain to your child why they are being evaluated. If you tell your child that they will be evaluated but do not explain why, they might get anxious or upset. This is a good opportunity to start talking about learning differences in a positive way.

   "A lot of kids get taken out of class for different reasons. I bet the other kids won't even notice. If you do choose to tell other kids why you're leaving class, I bet your friends will support you."

4. Set a positive tone for your child. No matter what the results of the evaluation, teach them never to be embarrassed because they learn differently.

   "We all know you're very smart, and this will help us understand the ways that you learn best. You may learn differently from other kids, but that in no way means that you aren't as smart as your friends. Never let anyone tell you otherwise!" Discuss activities that your child does well.

INVESTIGATION IN PROGRESS

5. Manage your own stress. Feel confident that you are doing the right thing! This problem- solving process will lead to knowledge and solutions.

6. The most critical piece of the evaluation is that you should walk away with a complete picture of how your child learns. That means you should: 1. have an understanding of your child's potential, and whether their academic and processing skills are consistent with their potential. What are your child's specific areas of strength and need? 2) understand the numbers and how they are reported and interpreted and 3) feel comfortable with the plan or "road map" that has been presented, based on your child's evaluation results. If you aren't understanding, ask questions and get clarification. It is imperative that you leave feeling you all can accomplish the goals!

Made in the USA
Columbia, SC
29 August 2024

41313669R00018